W9-BJS-778

Friends of the
Houston Public Library

Wretched Ruins

by Steven L. Stern

Consultant: Paul F. Johnston
Washington, D.C.

BEARPORT
PUBLISHING

New York, New York

Credits

Cover and Title Page, © Kateryna Govorushchenko/iStockphoto, © Emily Goodwin/Big Stock Photo, © Roy Simon/Fotolia, and © Eric Isselée/Fotolia; 4-5, © Phil Norton/Loop Images/Corbis; 6, © Michael S. Yamashita/Corbis; 7TL, © Kurt Scholz/SuperStock; 7BL, © Robert Harding Picture Library/SuperStock; 7R, © The Trustees of The British Museum/Art Resource, NY; 8, © Laurie Chamberlain/Corbis; 9, © Martin Gray/NGS Image Collection; 10, © Philip Baird/www.anthroarcheart.org; 11L, © Keith Dannemiller/Corbis; 11R, © Gianni Dagli Orti/The Art Archive/Picture Desk; 12, © Carmen Redondo/Corbis; 13, © Wolfgang Kaehler/Corbis; 14, © Adam Woolfitt/Robert Harding Picture Library/SuperStock; 15L, © Lee Pettet/iStockphoto; 15R, Courtesy Wessex Archaeology; 16, © age fotostock/SuperStock; 17R, © Stacey Gamez/iStockphoto; 17TL, © NordseeMuseum-Nissenhaus Husum, Germany; 17BL, © NordseeMuseum-Nissenhaus Husum, Germany; 18, © Leonardo Díaz Romero/age fotostock/SuperStock; 19L, © Charles Marden Fitch/SuperStock; 19R, © Erich Lessing/Art Resource, NY; 20, © John Elk III/Alamy; 21L, © James P. Blair/NGS Image Collection; 21R, © Russell Kord/Alamy; 22, © Nik Wheeler/Corbis; 23, © age fotostock/SuperStock; 24TL, © Keren Su/Corbis; 24BL, © Yann Arthus-Bertrand/Corbis; 24R, © Charles & Josette Lenars/Corbis; 25L, © Nick Saunders/Barbara Heller Photo Library, London/Art Resource, NY; 25R, © Yann Arthus-Bertrand/Corbis; 26, © Constantinos Pliakos/Alamy; 27, © Pixsmiths.co.uk; 31L, © Ivonne Wierink/Shutterstock; 31R, © Leksele/Shutterstock; 32, © CJPhoto/Shutterstock.

Publisher: Kenn Goin
Editorial Director: Adam Siegel
Creative Director: Spencer Brinker
Design: Dawn Beard Creative
Photo Researcher: Jennifer Bright

Library of Congress Cataloging-in-Publication Data

Stern, Steven L.
 Wretched ruins / by Steven L. Stern.
     p. cm. — (Scary places)
 Includes bibliographical references and index.
 ISBN-13: 978-1-936087-55-6 (library binding)
 ISBN-10: 1-936087-55-3 (library binding)
 1. Antiquities—Juvenile literature. 2. Civilization, Ancient—Juvenile literature. 3. Historic sites—Juvenile literature. 4. Excavations (Archaeology)—Juvenile literature. 5. Archaeology—Juvenile literature. I. Title.
 CC171.S74 2010
 930.1—dc22

                                2009043980

Copyright © 2010 Bearport Publishing Company, Inc. All rights reserved. No part of this publication may be reproduced in whole or in part, stored in a retrieval system, or transmitted in any form or by any means, electronic, mechanical, photocopying, recording, or otherwise, without written permission from the publisher.

For more information, write to Bearport Publishing Company, Inc., 45 West 21st Street, Suite 3B, New York, New York, 10010. Printed in the United States of America.

10 9 8 7 6 5 4

Contents

Wretched Ruins 4

Dying for Their Ruler 6

The Lost City 8

Human Hearts for the Sun God 10

The Hidden City of Tombs 12

The Ring of Stones 14

A City Beneath the Sea 16

Bloody Rituals in the Jungle 18

The Stone Giants 20

Victims for the God of Rain 22

Strange Figures in the Desert 24

Gateway to the Underworld 26

Wretched Ruins Around the World 28

Glossary 30

Bibliography 31

Read More 31

Learn More Online 31

Index 32

About the Author 32

Wretched Ruins

In the shadows of history lurk the remains of **ancient** nations and powerful kingdoms. Many of these civilizations disappeared hundreds—or even thousands—of years ago. Yet ghostly traces of their world linger on in the **ruins** of their crumbling buildings, silent **tombs**, and blood-stained **pyramids**. These mysterious links to the past offer clues to strange, and even shocking, events.

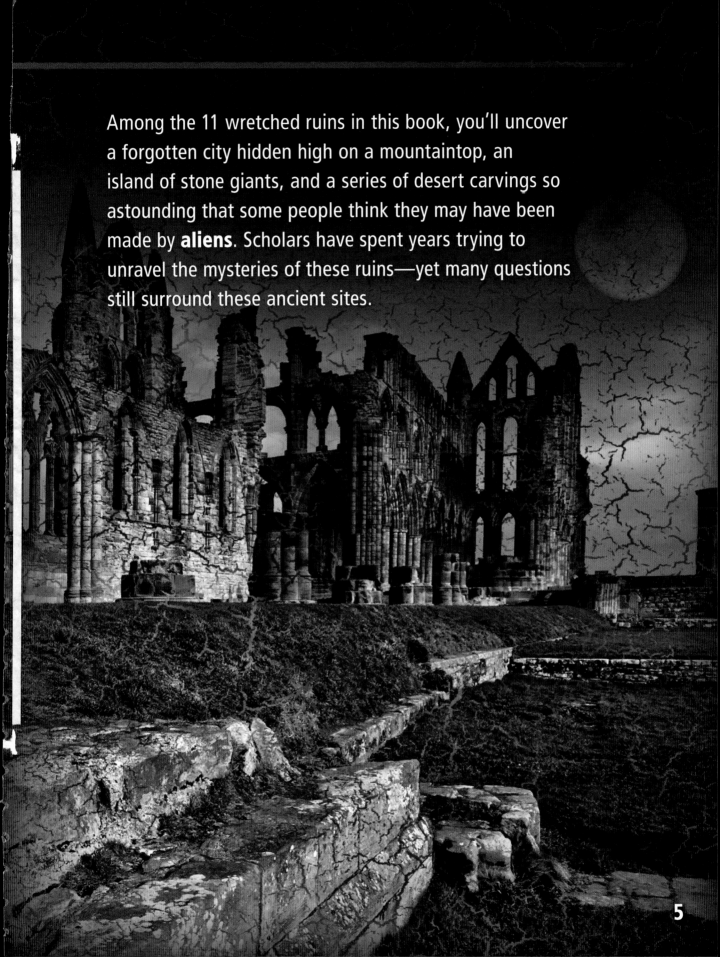

Among the 11 wretched ruins in this book, you'll uncover a forgotten city hidden high on a mountaintop, an island of stone giants, and a series of desert carvings so astounding that some people think they may have been made by **aliens**. Scholars have spent years trying to unravel the mysteries of these ruins—yet many questions still surround these ancient sites.

Dying for Their Ruler

Ur, Iraq

Ur was one of the world's earliest cities. About 5,000 years ago, it was located in the region of Sumer (SOO-muhr), in what is now Iraq. At its center was a giant pyramid called a ziggurat. It was built as a **temple** for the moon god, Nanna. Not far from the temple was Ur's royal **burial ground**. Unfortunately, when a ruler was laid to rest there, others from the city were killed and buried there as well.

Temple built for the moon god, Nanna

In the 1920s, British **archaeologist** Leonard Woolley discovered Ur's royal burial ground. In these rooms carved out deep in the ground, he found the **corpses** of Sumerian kings and queens. The **graves** contained beautiful works of art and many silver and gold objects. They also revealed some disturbing facts about Sumerian **rituals**.

Close by the kings and queens lay the skeletons of their servants, soldiers, and musicians. Some rulers had been buried with more than 70 royal **attendants**. Many of them were young, and near each one was a gold or clay cup. The cups had been filled with a poisonous liquid. After the attendants had finished their deadly drink, they lay down to be buried with their ruler. The bodies looked like they had curled up to sleep.

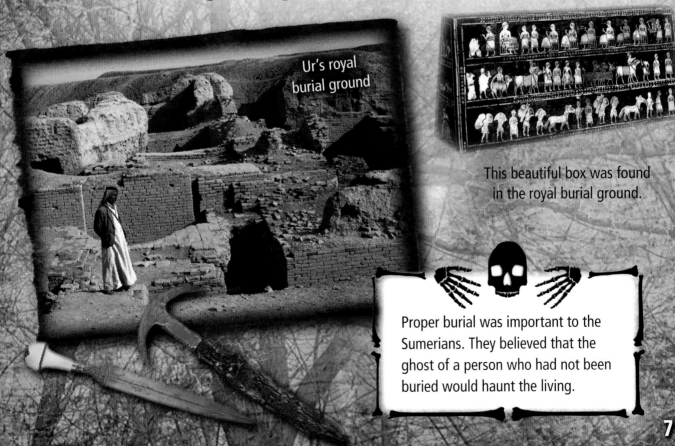

Ur's royal burial ground

This beautiful box was found in the royal burial ground.

Proper burial was important to the Sumerians. They believed that the ghost of a person who had not been buried would haunt the living.

The Lost City

Machu Picchu, Peru

The Inca were the most powerful people in South America during the 1400s. Their massive empire stretched some 2,500 miles (4,023 km) from the present-day country of Ecuador to present-day Chile. In 1532, Spanish soldiers conquered the Inca. They destroyed many beautiful Incan buildings. Yet one of the Inca's most splendid cities, Machu Picchu (MAH-choo PEE-choo), remained safe, hidden high on a mountaintop. Would it ever be found again?

Machu Picchu

In 1911, American explorer Hiram Bingham set off for Peru. He wanted to study Incan ruins. A villager told him of a secret city high up in the Andes (AN-deez) Mountains. Was the story true? To find out, Bingham climbed up a steep mountainside covered by thick jungle. When he finally reached the top, 8,000 feet (2.4 km) up, he was amazed.

There before him was a city that had been hidden from the outside world for 400 years. Poking through the clouds were about 200 buildings, including temples, palaces, and houses. Heavy blocks of gray granite had been perfectly cut to create the buildings. Yet the Inca had no wheeled carts or iron tools. How could they have moved and shaped such large stones?

There was another puzzling question. What had happened to the people of Machu Picchu? Had they all been killed by another tribe? Had they died of some disease? The answer is as hard to find as the city itself.

The Intihuatana stone

The Intihuatana is a **sacred** stone at Machu Picchu dedicated to the Incan sun god. According to **legend**, some people could connect with the **spirit** world by touching their foreheads to the stone.

Human Hearts for the Sun God

Tenochtitlán, Mexico

In the 1400s and early 1500s, the Aztec people had a vast empire in what is today Mexico. Its capital was Tenochtitlán (*tay*-nohch-TEET-lahn). Spanish soldiers led by Hernán Cortés conquered the Aztec in 1521. They built Mexico City, the present-day capital of Mexico, over the ruins of Tenochtitlán. Yet even today, there are grim reminders of the Aztec's bloody past.

Tenochtitlán

The splendid city of Tenochtitlán was built on an island in Lake Texcoco. There were white stone palaces and temples, houses, and gardens. Most main streets were **canals**, which people traveled on by canoe. In the heart of the city stood the Templo Mayor. This building was about 90 feet (27 m) tall. At its top were twin temples, which honored two Aztec gods.

The city was beautiful, but it had a dark side. Each year Aztec priests **sacrificed** thousands of people to win the favor of their sun god, Huitzilopochtli (*wee*-tsee-loh-POHCH-tlee). Most victims were prisoners of war. They were led to the top of Huitzilopochtli's pyramid. There, the priests would cut out their still-beating hearts! When Cortés first came to Tenochtitlán in 1519, he told one of his men to count the skulls of recent victims. The man claimed to have counted 136,000 skulls!

After sacrificing their victims, the Aztec priests threw the bloody bodies off the pyramid. Then the heads were cut off and stuck onto a *tzompantli*, or skull rack.

A wall of carved skulls at the Templo Mayor

The Hidden City of Tombs

Petra, Jordan

More than 2,000 years ago, an Arab people called the Nabataeans settled in Petra (PEE-truh), a desert city surrounded by mountains. Petra became a trade center and home to more than 20,000 people. Over time, however, trade routes changed. The city became less important, and the Nabataeans moved away. Petra was all but forgotten by the outside world. For more than 500 years, no one but the region's **Bedouin** people set eyes on the mysterious city.

Tombs carved into the cliffs of Petra

Swiss explorer Johann Ludwig Burckhardt was traveling to Cairo in 1812. He heard rumors of an ancient city lost in the desert sand. The city was said to be hidden from sight by mountains. Could it be real? Burckhardt paid two Bedouin guides to lead him there. They took him to a long, narrow pass between towering rock walls. When Burckhardt stepped out into the sunlight, he was stunned.

Pale red sandstone cliffs surrounded him. Carved into the cliffs were tombs, temples, burial chambers, and theaters. The Nabataeans had created these structures about two thousand years before. Some of the carved tombs honored their gods. Others were built to remember the dead. Some, however, were tombs for criminals—where they had been buried alive!

Around 400,000 people visit Petra each year. The site has even been used as a movie set. Yet even today, the only way to enter the hidden city is by foot, horse, or camel.

The Ring of Stones

Stonehenge, England

On a misty plain in southern England stands an eerie sight. Huge gray stones, some weighing 25 tons (23 metric tons), are arranged in a circle. The towering stone **monument**, called Stonehenge, was built by people who lived in the area thousands of years ago. What drove these ancient people to undertake such a difficult task? That is just one of the many mysteries surrounding Stonehenge.

Stonehenge

Around 3100 B.C. people in southern England began building an unusual monument. They brought gigantic stones, some of which were from areas up to 240 miles (386 km) away, and placed them in a circle. The work was slow and tiring. It was done in stages over 1,500 years. What were the people trying to build? No one knows for sure.

Some people believe Stonehenge was a temple where people came for religious ceremonies. Others think it was an **observatory** used to look at the sun, moon, and stars. Or it may have had other purposes . . . .

Sick and injured people may have traveled to Stonehenge, believing that the stones had magical healing powers. Others may have come to connect with the spirits of the dead. Indeed, on a quiet evening, some say the murmurs of spirits can still be heard.

Recent evidence indicates that Stonehenge was an ancient burial ground. It is estimated that up to 240 people are buried there. That would make it the largest known cemetery of its time in England.

A City Beneath the Sea

Rungholt, Germany

In January 1362, a fierce storm swept across southern England. The wind caused massive waves in the North Sea. Powerful floods swamped the Danish, German, and Dutch coasts. Thousands died, including every person in one town that vanished into the sea.

The disaster of 1362 became known as the "Great Drowning of Men." A witness wrote, "A strong **gale** blew from the north so violently for a day and night that it flattened trees, mills, houses, and a great many church towers." Between 25,000 and 100,000 people were killed by the fierce storm.

No place was harder hit than the **port** of Rungholt on the island of Strand in Germany. This bustling town of 1,500 people sank almost without a trace. In the 1920s and 1930s, remains of the once-booming town were found. Although most of the city still lies buried below the sea, according to legend one can still hear the church bells of Rungholt ringing through the area on a stormy night.

These objects were found near Rungholt.

In 1634, the island of Strand was struck another deadly blow when a powerful storm swept away large parts of the island.

Bloody Rituals in the Jungle

Tikal, Guatemala

In 1848, explorers working for the Guatemalan government hacked their way through the steaming tropical jungle. Spider monkeys danced in the trees. Jaguars hid in the green shadows. Suddenly, the explorers saw the top of a tall stone structure poking through the trees. They had found the ruins of the once-great Mayan city of Tikal (tee-KAHL).

Tikal

From about 250 A.D. to about 900 A.D., the Maya had a great civilization in Central America and Mexico. They created beautiful buildings and works of art. They studied the stars and planets. They also developed an advanced writing system and a yearly calendar.

At the center of this world was Tikal—a city of temples, palaces, and giant stone pyramids. It was here that the Maya carried out their sacred rituals. They killed turkeys, dogs, and other animals to win the favor of their gods. They also sacrificed humans, taking the lives of prisoners, slaves, and even children.

About 1,300 years ago, more than 50,000 people lived in Tikal and the surrounding areas. By the end of the tenth century, however, the city had mysteriously become a ghost town. Before long, the jungle covered Tikal, hiding its bloody secrets.

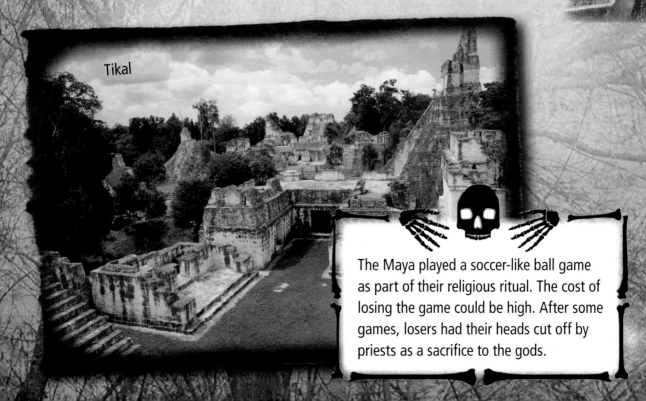

Tikal

The Maya played a soccer-like ball game as part of their religious ritual. The cost of losing the game could be high. After some games, losers had their heads cut off by priests as a sacrifice to the gods.

The Stone Giants

Easter Island, Chile

Easter Island is one of the most out-of-the-way places on Earth. It is located far out in the South Pacific Ocean, about 2,180 miles (3,508 km) west of Chile. The island is only about 63 square miles (163 sq km), about the size of Washington, D.C. Yet somehow hundreds of stone giants began appearing on the island around 1,000 years ago. How did they get there?

Easter Island

The first Europeans landed on Easter Island in the 1700s. What they saw stopped them in their tracks. Hundreds of frightening stone statues stared down at them. Some were more than 30 feet (9 m) tall and weighed over 80 tons (73 metric tons).

Between about 1200 and 1650, ancient **Polynesian** people had built more than 800 of these statues to honor their **ancestors**. The statues were called *moai* (mo-EYE). Using only simple tools, the Easter Islanders somehow were able to create the giants and move them onto great stone platforms.

War between groups of islanders broke out around 1680. Attacks grew more and more bloody. The groups even ate their dead enemies. They tried to destroy one another's moai. By the early 1800s, nearly all the statues had been knocked down. More than a hundred years later, archaeologists raised some of the fallen statues. Today, these stone giants, grimly silent, once again watch over Easter Island.

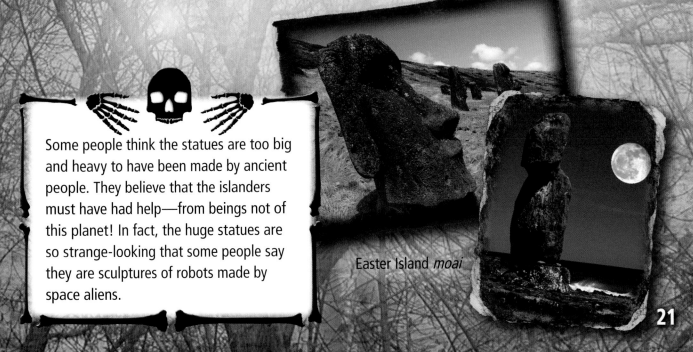

Easter Island *moai*

Some people think the statues are too big and heavy to have been made by ancient people. They believe that the islanders must have had help—from beings not of this planet! In fact, the huge statues are so strange-looking that some people say they are sculptures of robots made by space aliens.

Victims for the God of Rain

Chichén Itzá, Mexico

In southeastern Mexico stand the ruins of Chichén Itzá (chee-CHEN eet-SAH). Stone temples, pyramids, and other buildings offer clues about the people who lived there more than 1,000 years ago. Many chilling stories are told about the city. Are they fact or fiction? The bones of the victims tell the tale.

Chichén Itzá

Archaeologists do not all agree on Chichén Itzá's history. They know that the city was Mayan. However, other ancient people, such as the powerful **Toltecs**, may also have lived there. What archaeologists do agree on is that Chichén Itzá was a sacred place as well as a city of death.

Inside the city of Chichén Itzá was the sacred well, or cenote (sin-OH-tee). The round cavern was about 213 feet (65 m) wide and 110 feet (33.5 m) deep. No one drank the water, however. Instead, people came here to make offerings to Chac, the Mayan god of rain and lightning.

Water was scarce, and people needed rain to grow crops. So they offered Chac gold, copper, **jade**—and human sacrifices. The living victims were thrown into the well. When archaeologists **excavated** the well, they found hundreds of bones. Many were from the skeletons of children.

The sacred well

The Maya believed that the dead went down to a dark underworld called Xibalba. The cenote was a gateway to this underworld.

23

Strange Figures in the Desert

Nazca, Peru

Airplanes first began flying over the Peruvian desert in the 1920s. People aboard looked down and gasped. Far below, carved into the dry soil, were hundreds of lines and figures. Who made these amazing drawings? Gods? Aliens? Giants?

Drawings found at Nazca

Scientists came to the Peruvian desert to investigate the mysterious drawings. They found hundreds of lines and pictures. Someone had created the drawings by scraping away reddish-brown desert stones to expose the yellow soil underneath. There were pictures of birds, a spider, and even a monkey. They were gigantic. One drawing of a lizard was bigger than two soccer fields!

About 2,000 years ago, the Nazca (NAHS-kuh) people lived in this desert area. Could they have carved these figures? If so, why would they make them so large that they could be clearly seen only from above?

Among the pictures of animals and plants, scientists also found images of strange beings. One figure had two huge hands—one of which had only four fingers. Another figure, about 100 feet (30.4 m) tall, looked like a man with huge eyes. Is it possible that these were drawings of creatures that had visited Earth in the time of the Nazca?

Some people believe that the drawings are landing strips for returning aliens. Why else can they be seen only from the sky?

Gateway to the Underworld

Parga, Greece

In 1958, archaeologist Sotirios Dakaris discovered the ruins of a stone building in northwestern Greece, near the town of Parga. It was a temple more than 2,000 years old. More remarkable, however, was the gloomy chamber that Dakaris found underneath the temple. Dakaris had stumbled upon the Nekromanteio—a dark place where the living met the dead.

Ancient ruins near Parga, Greece

The ancient Greeks believed that the **souls** of the dead went down to the underworld, called Hades (HAY-deez). The souls entered Hades through certain caves and other openings in the rocky ground. The chamber that Dakaris had found was such an entrance. In ancient times, visitors dared to go there in hopes of getting advice from the dead—who the ancient Greeks believed were able to foretell the future.

A priest led trembling visitors through the spooky underground darkness. He guided them through prayers and magical rituals before they were allowed to meet with the dead souls. Afterward, the visitors were warned not to talk about their experience. They did as they were told. The penalty for breaking their silence was death.

Underground passage below the temple

To prepare for meeting the dead, visitors ate special foods provided by the priests. These included beans, pork, and bread. They also made offerings, such as blood from a sheep.

Wretched Ruins

NORTH AMERICA

SOUTH AMERICA

Pacific Ocean

Atlantic Ocean

Tenochtitlán, Mexico

Human sacrifices in a beautiful city

Chichén Itzá, Mexico

Human sacrifices to please the rain god

Tikal, Guatemala

Sacred ceremonies of blood

Machu Picchu, Peru

A city hidden high on a mountaintop

Easter Island, Chile

Giant statues on a faraway island

Nazca, Peru

Mysterious carvings in the desert

Around the World

Stonehenge, England

An ancient circle of huge gray stones

Rungholt, Germany

A city beneath the sea

Arctic Ocean

ASIA

EUROPE

Ur, Iraq

Burial ground of Sumerian kings and queens

Parga, Greece

A gateway to the underworld

Indian Ocean

Petra, Jordan

A city of tombs, lost in the desert

AFRICA

Pacific Ocean

AUSTRALIA

N

W E

S

Southern Ocean

ANTARCTICA

29

Glossary

aliens (AY-lee-uhnz) creatures from outer space

ancestors (AN-sess-turz) family members who lived a long time ago

ancient (AYN-shunt) very old

archaeologist (*ar*-kee-OL-uh-jist) a scientist who learns about ancient times by studying things he or she digs up, such as old buildings, tools, and pottery

attendants (uh-TEN-duhnts) servants

Bedouin (BED-oo-in) Arab people of the desert regions of the Middle East

burial ground (BER-ee-uhl GROUND) an area of land where dead bodies are buried

canals (kuh-NALZ) human-made waterways for boats

corpses (KORPS-iz) dead bodies

excavated (EKS-kuh-*vay*-tid) uncovered by digging

gale (GAYL) a strong wind

graves (GRAYVZ) holes dug into the ground where dead people are buried

jade (JAYD) a green stone used for making jewelry and ornaments

legend (LEJ-uhnd) a story that is handed down from the past that may be based on fact but is not always completely true

monument (MON-yoo-muhnnt) a structure built to honor a person or event

observatory (uhb-ZUR-vuh-*tor*-ee) a place or building for viewing stars and planets

Polynesian (*pol*-uh-NEE-zhuhn) relating to islands in the Pacific Ocean or the people from there

port (PORT) a place where ships load and unload cargo

pyramids (PIHR-uh-midz) stone monuments having a square base and triangular sides that meet at a point on top

rituals (RICH-oo-uhlz) special ceremonies for religious or other purposes

ruins (ROO-inz) what is left of something that has decayed or been destroyed

sacred (SAY-krid) holy, religious

sacrificed (SAK-ruh-fyest) killed a person or animal as part of a ceremony or as an offering to a god

souls (SOHLZ) the spirits of people who have died

spirit (SPIHR-it) a supernatural creature, such as a ghost

temple (TEM-puhl) a religious building where people worship

Toltecs (TOHL-teks) people of a Native American empire in Mexico that existed during the 900s through the 1100s

tombs (TOOMZ) rooms or buildings for the dead

Bibliography

Bahn, Paul G., ed. *Lost Cities.* New York: Welcome Rain (1999).

Ingpen, Robert R., and Philip Wilkinson. *Encyclopedia of Mysterious Places: The Life and Legends of Ancient Sites Around the World.* New York: Viking Studio Books (1990).

Reader's Digest Editors. *Vanished Civilizations: The Hidden Secrets of Lost Cities and Forgotten Peoples.* London: Reader's Digest Association (2002).

Westwood, Jennifer, ed. *Mysterious Places: The World's Unexplained Symbolic Sites, Ancient Cities and Lost Lands.* New York: Barnes & Noble Books (1998).

Wilkinson, Philip, and Michael Pollard. *The Master Builders.* New York: Chelsea House Publishers (1994).

Read More

Hoobler, Dorothy and Thomas. *Lost Civilizations.* New York: Walker and Company (1992).

Hook, Jason. *Lost Cities.* Austin, TX: Raintree Steck-Vaughn Publishers (2002).

Morris, Neil. *Lost Cities.* North Mankato, MN: Smart Apple Media (2008).

Learn More Online

To learn more about ancient ruins, visit
www.bearportpublishing.com/ScaryPlaces

Index

Aztec 10–11

Bedouins 12–13
Bingham, Hiram 9
Burckhardt, Johann Ludwig 13

cenote 23
Chichén Itzá, Mexico 22–23, 28
Cortés, Hernán 10–11

Dakaris, Sotirios 26–27

Easter Island, Chile 20–21, 28

Inca 8–9

Machu Picchu, Peru 8–9, 28
Maya 18–19, 23
moai 21

Nabataeans 12–13
Nazca, Peru 24–25, 28
Nekromanteio 26

Parga, Greece 26–27, 29
Petra, Jordan 12–13, 29

Rungholt, Germany 16–17, 29

sacrifices 11, 19, 23, 28
Stonehenge, England 14–15, 29

Tenochtitlán, Mexico 10–11, 28
Tikal, Guatemala 18–19, 28
Toltecs 23

Ur, Iraq 6–7, 29

Woolley, Leonard 7

ziggurat 6

About the Author

Steven L. Stern has more than 30 years of experience as a writer and editor, developing textbooks, learning materials, and works of nonfiction and fiction for children and adults. He is the author of 19 books as well as numerous articles and short stories. He has also worked as a teacher, a lexicographer, and a writing consultant.

930.1 S   HOAKX
Stern, Steven L.
Wretched ruins /

OAK FOREST
01/13